INTRODUCTION

Sweet Teacher Friends,

We are excited to help you dive deeper into God's Word this Christmas. Before we get too far, there are a few things we would like you to know.

First, allow us to introduce ourselves for those who do not know us.

Bonnie was born and raised in a rural Georgia town. Studying at Southeastern Baptist Theological Seminary brought her to North Carolina. During her time at seminary, she studied Women's Ministry, but God had a slightly different plan for her to teach in a local kindergarten classroom. If you want to get to know Bonnie more, follow her on Instagram: @bonniekathryn

Bethany was born and raised in a small town in Virginia. She studied Communications and Women's Ministry at Liberty University. From 2007-2016, she was living the city life in Florida. In 2016, she moved to North Carolina to teach middle and high school English. Though English is a passion, Bible trumps even her love for grammar...and y'all, that's big! If you want to get to know Bethany more, follow her on Instagram: @theenglishnerd

Secondly, let's talk logistics for a minute.

We will be using the English Standard Version throughout this reading plan. When we ask you questions, the ESV will help you to answer these questions. If you do not have an ESV Bible, you can use the online version found at www.esv.org. With that said, you may use any version you choose. You just may find that the wording in other versions does not match the wording in our questions.

We have designed this reading plan in Chronological Order - the order that the events happened in history. You will notice that Chronological Order is different than the order we find in our Bibles. We pray that this helps you see these sometimes all too familiar events in a way that you have not viewed them previously.

Lastly, let us share a little bit about our heart behind this plan.

If you've joined us in the past, we have done Bible studies: *Grace Changes Everything* and *Fruited*. In these studies, we have included our commentary as we walked with you through Ephesians and Galatians. As every good teacher knows, there is a time and place for walking our students through material, but there also comes a time for letting go and letting them tackle the learned skills themselves. You are our students. We are ready to watch you shine! (No worries! If this is your first time with us, you can totally rock this plan, too!)

One of the main goals of Teachers in the Word is to spur you, a teacher, to be in the Word. While there is a time and place for studies, there is also a time and place for sitting down with our Bibles, opening them, and allowing the Holy Spirit to guide us into understanding of His Word. What better time than Christmas to allow Him to help us as we dive into Scriptures that give us a glimpse into the night of that precious Baby's birth.

The first time a teacher releases her students to try a task on their own, struggles are expected. It's new. It's different. It's challenging. That's okay. In fact, that's normal. Teachers, hear us: you are the student. You will struggle. You will find some of this material challenging. That's okay! Don't be like some of our beloved students who get frustrated and shut down, never to return. We have one word for you: persevere. If you hit a passage that you do not understand, we beg you to do what Psalm 1:2 says and meditate on it. Meditate comes from a Hebrew word that literally means "to chew the cud"...yes, like a cow! The Holy Spirit knows how much we can handle, and when He knows that we are ready to digest and understand a portion of Scripture, He will open our eyes to it. In the meantime, it is our job to continue reading and studying and meditating on challenging passages. There may be questions asked of you that you don't immediately understand or for which you don't have an answer. Read them, think on them, skip over them for a time, go back to them. We know as teachers that there is learning that happens IN the struggle, so it's okay to struggle. Struggle. Meditate. Persevere.

Our prayer is that this reading plan will challenge you as you come to adore Christ more this Christmas.

Bethany   *Bonnie Kathryn*

HOW TO USE QR CODES

We both use QR codes in our classroom. QR codes are a fun way to make learning tech-based and interactive. Bethany uses QR codes for self-check in her centers. It helps her to avoid having 20 questions during an activity. It is a great way for students to self-assess. Bonnie uses QR codes for write-the-room activities, listening-to-reading activities, and to show how-to videos for handwriting. She begins the school year teaching her five-year-olds about QR codes and how to use them on the class iPads. We believe that if Bonnie's kindergarten students can use a QR code reader, you can, too!

 **Step 1**

You will want to download a FREE QR code reader app on your iPad, iPhone, or Android phone. Do not pay for one. There are SO many free options that work well. If you find that one is acting quirky, delete it, and pick another free option. If you have a newly updated iPhone and/or iPad, open your camera and hold it over the code. The weblink will pop up on your screen.

 **Step 2**

Open your newly downloaded QR code reader app. You will need to give it access to your camera. It will prompt you.

 **Step 3**

The app will have a square box that you will hold over the QR code. It should scan immediately, and it will take you to the QR code link. Essentially, the QR code links to different webpages. Throughout this reading plan, our QR codes are linked to videos.

 **Step 4**

Try it out here:

Disclaimer: We do not own the rights to any outside links that are included. The QR codes and bit.ly links are simply to be used as a resource and are considered bonus material, not main content. Because we do not own them, we have no control over what the original owner does with the link. If a link or QR code becomes inactive, we are unable to fix this issue. You can search the song title and/or artist and find a similar version.

HOW TO STUDY THE BIBLE

We get it - studying the Bible can seem like a daunting task...especially if you're new to this whole Bible study thing. The last thing we want is for you to become so overwhelmed by questions like "Where do I start?" and "What do I even do?" and "How do I understand what I'm reading?" that you give up all too soon. So, let us share two study methods with you that we find simplistic, practical, and rewarding.

These methods are not magical, of course, but they do help you know where to begin. Use one or use both - it's totally up to you.

THE H.E.A.R. METHOD

Highlight: Read and observe everything in the passage

Examine: Based on your reading, discover what the passage means in its context by reading what's around the verses

Apply: Understand how the meaning of the passage affects your life personally

Respond: Pray God's Word back to Him, asking to believe, share, and put the Bible into practice in your life and your relationships

THE HAND METHOD

As you read, look for things that are...

HOW DO I KNOW JESUS?

One of the most important questions that you could ask is this one: how do I know Jesus? Friend, we do not want to go any further before we make sure that we have told you how to meet our Precious Savior. Let's take a little journey down the Romans Road. Paul is a great guide for this journey.

- **Romans 3:23** "For all have sinned and fall short of the glory of God."
  - You see, not a single one of us is perfect and sinless. We were all born sinners in need of a Savior. We are all in this together - mud-stained sinners we are.
  - God cannot stand in the presence of sin because He is holy. We fall short of being able to see His glory because of our sin.

- **Romans 6:23** "For the wages of sin is death, but the free gift of God is eternal life in Christ Jesus our Lord."
  - To repair our relationship with this holy God, we must pay for our sins. The Bible is clear that the payment due for sin is death. Not the grandest news, right? But wait...next verse on this Romans Road...

- **Romans 5:8** "But God shows His love for us in that while we were still sinners, Christ died for us."
  - Praise Jesus that He came to this earth as a baby with one goal in mind: to die a sinner's death on the cross for us, and the Bible says that He endured this cross with joy because He knew it would bring us salvation! He paid our debt! His gift to us is free to us! We simply must receive it.

- **Romans 10:13** "For everyone who calls on the name of the Lord will be saved."
  - Sound too simple? Accepting Jesus as your Savior isn't meant to be complicated. It's simply a matter of bowing your will to His and telling Him you want Him to be Lord over your life, you want Him to be in charge.

- **Romans 10:9-10** "Because, if you confess with your mouth that Jesus is Lord and believe in your heart that God raised Him from the dead, you will be saved. For with the heart one believes and is justified, and with the mouth one confesses and is saved."
  - It's as simple as that: believe and confess that belief. Believe that Jesus is Who He says He is and that He died for you, but He didn't stay dead because God the Father raised Him from the dead, so He could offer us eternal life. Jesus conquered death. Confess that you believe that He did that for you.

If you are choosing right now in this moment to accept Jesus as the Lord of your life, as your Savior, would you tell someone? Find a friend, a pastor, a family member, and let them know about the decision you just made.

Friend, welcome to the family! We are excited for you as you begin to build your relationship with Jesus!

There is no better way to begin to build your relationship with Him that than to dive into His Word this Christmas season as we walk through Jesus' life in the pages of Scripture. We pray that you will see these Scriptures in a different light now knowing that you are His.

DECEMBER 1ST

- [ ] Romans 5:3-5
- [ ] Romans 8:24-25
- [ ] Romans 15:12-13

RESPOND & REFLECT

1. Trace Paul's process of hope. How do we see hope produced in our lives?

2. According to Paul in 8:24-25, what is hope NOT?

3. In 15:12-13, Whose coming did Isaiah prophesy that would bring hope to the Gentiles (the non-Jews, who currently did not have access to the Gospel)?

4. How can we abound in hope, according to Paul?

BECAUSE OF Jesus WE HAVE HOPE

DECEMBER 2ND

☐ Isaiah 1:18

http://bit.ly/ADOREocomeemmanuel

RESPOND & REFLECT

1. Ultimately, what is being promised in this verse?

2. Isaiah 1 is filled with words like "rebelled" (vs. 2), "sinful nation" (vs. 4), and "burden" (vs. 14). Knowing this chapter is the LORD's accusation against Judah's wickedness, how would this promise in verse 18 shock and simultaneously encourage them?

DECEMBER 3RD

Isaiah 9:6

Isaiah 11:1-9

http://bit.ly/ADORElightoftheworld

RESPOND & REFLECT

1. The prophecy in 9:6 was spoken approximately 700 years prior to Jesus' birth. Do you think that the people in Isaiah's time fully grasped Who he was describing to them? Explain.

2. Isaiah 11:1 references the "shoot from the stump of Jesse" just like Romans 15:12-13 did (from December 1st). We know, of course, these references are to Jesus. Look in verses 2-5 of chapter 11. List three things that stand out to you that Isaiah prophesies about Jesus.

DECEMBER 4TH

☐ Micah 5:2-5a

http://bit.ly/ADORElittletownofbethlehem

RESPOND & REFLECT

1. Why do you think God chose a city "too little to be among the clans of Judah" to be His Son's earthly birthplace? What might that say about the message God the Father was sending to those people and to us today?

2. Shepherd life was a lowly, lonely life. Despite those descriptives, how does Micah turn that shepherd life upside down in verse 4? How does he say that this coming Shepherd will rule? (Hint: It is a word that they for sure wouldn't have connected with shepherd life!)

3. In verse 5a (the very beginning part), what did Micah say Jesus would be for them?

DECEMBER 5TH

☐ Luke 1:5-25

http://bit.ly/ADOREgloryinhighest

RESPOND & REFLECT

1. What kind of people were Elizabeth and Zechariah according to Luke (verses 5-6)?

2. What did the angel tell Zechariah when he appeared to him (verse 13)?

3. What was John's job going to be (verses 16-17)?

DECEMBER 6TH

☐ Luke 1:26-38

http://bit.ly/ADOREgloria

RESPOND & REFLECT

1. Gabriel, the same angel that appeared to Zechariah, appears to whom in this portion of Scripture?

2. What is the age gap between John the Baptist (Elizabeth's son) and Jesus? (Hint: Look at verses 26 and 36 for help.) Why do you think God the Father chose to allow their births to be so close together?

3. Although stunned by the news that Gabriel brought her, what is Mary's ultimate response to this announcement (verse 38)?

DECEMBER 7TH

Take time today for rest and reflection. If you need to catch up in the reading plan, today would be a good day for that. You can use the box below to jot down things that God has shown you in His word this week.

this week...

IN HIM we have REST

DECEMBER 8TH

- [ ] Psalm 85:8
- [ ] Psalm 29:11
- [ ] Isaiah 26:3
- [ ] Isaiah 26:12
- [ ] Isaiah 54:10
- [ ] John 14:27
- [ ] Philippians 4:6-7

http://bit.ly/ADOREharktheherald

RESPOND & REFLECT

1. What is the theme - the common thread - running through all of these verses?

2. According to Isaiah 26:3, what 2 steps must we take in order to have "perfect peace"?

3. Is there anything we can do to make the LORD remove His covenant of peace with us according to Isaiah 54:10?

4. Instead of worrying and becoming anxious, what does Philippians 4:6 tell us to do?

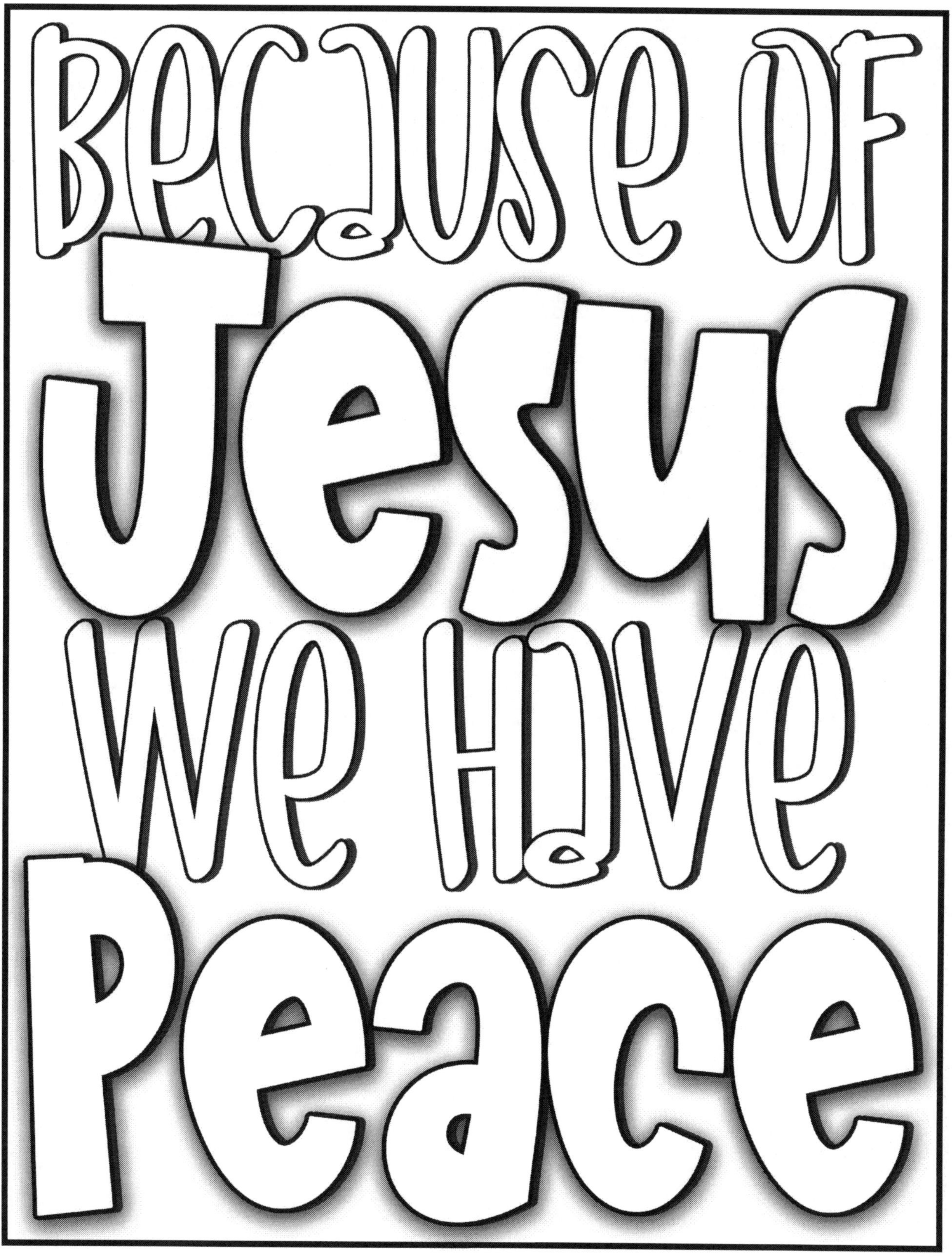
Because of
Jesus
We have
Peace

DECEMBER 9TH

Luke 1:39-56

http://bit.ly/ADOREuntous

RESPOND & REFLECT

1. What happened the moment that Mary greeted Elizabeth?

2. Verses 46-55 are known as Mary's Song of Praise. What does Mary acknowledge about God in verse 47? In other words, Who is He to her?

3. Verses 54-55 highlight the reason that God the Father sent His Son into a sinful world, despite the sinfulness of Israel. (Remember Isaiah 1?) What caused the Father to keep His promise to such sinful humans, to whom we also belong?

DECEMBER 10TH

Luke 1:57-66

http://bit.ly/ADOREoholynight

RESPOND & REFLECT

1. What did people expect Zechariah and Elizabeth to name their child? Why?

2. What did they name him instead? Why?

3. What loosed Zechariah's lips, allowing him to speak again?

DECEMBER 11TH

Luke 1:67-80

http://bit.ly/ADOREmarydidyouknow

RESPOND & REFLECT

1. Zechariah's prophecy in these verses echoes Mary's Song of Praise. Look specifically at verses 72-73. Why did God the Father send His Son into the world?

2. What does Zechariah prophesy about his son, John, in verses 76-77?

3. According to verse 79, who is Jesus coming to rescue? Be specific.

BORN to set thy people FREE

DECEMBER 12TH

☐ John 1:1-18

http://bit.ly/ADOREnoel

RESPOND & REFLECT

1. If the Word is one of Jesus' names, what does verse 2 teach us about Jesus and His existence?

2. Who is verses 6-8 talking about? Be specific.

3. Look at the first 9 words of verse 14. What significance do those words have? Why does their meaning hold such monumental value?

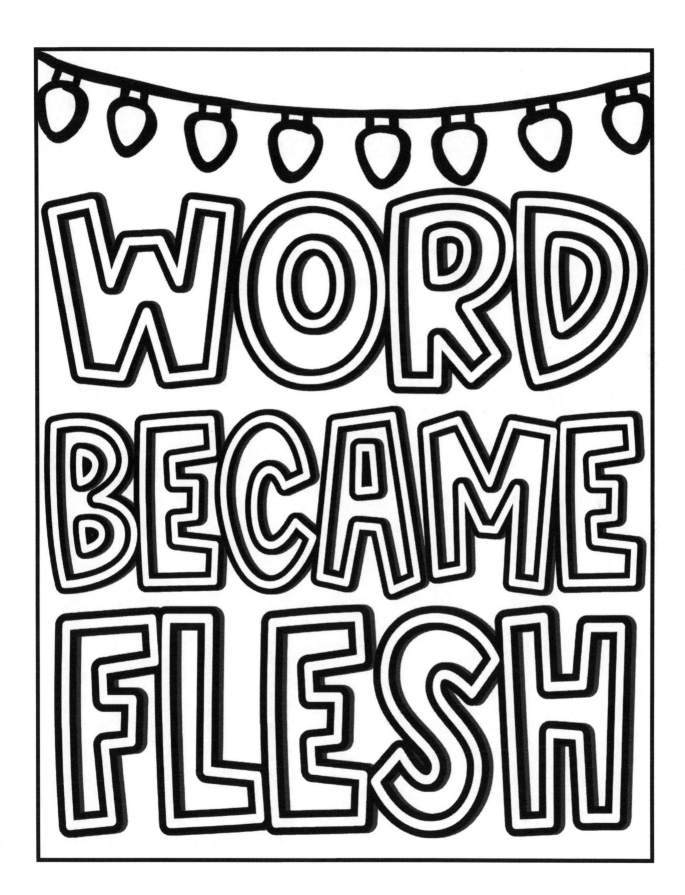

DECEMBER 13TH

Matthew 1:18-25

http://bit.ly/ADOREheshallreign

RESPOND & REFLECT

1. According to Matthew, what kind of man was Joseph (verse 19)?

2. What does Immanuel mean?

3. Why would Immanuel be a comforting idea to them?

4. Although the angel's plans caused Joseph's plans to be completely altered, how did he respond to what he was told to do?

and you shall call his name

JESUS

DECEMBER 14TH

Take time today for rest and reflection. If you need to catch up in the reading plan, today would be a good day for that. You can use the box below to jot down things that God has shown you in His word this week.

this week...

IN HIM we have REST

DECEMBER 15TH

☐ Psalm 30:5

☐ 1 Peter 1:8-9

RESPOND & REFLECT

1. What word do you see repeated in both of these verses?

2. What comfort can we take away from Psalm 30:5?

3. According to 1 Peter 1:8-9, why do we rejoice with inexpressible joy? (Hint: Verse 9 offers the answer.)

BECAUSE OF JESUS WE HAVE JOY

DECEMBER 16TH

☐ Matthew 2

http://bit.ly/ADOREadorehim

RESPOND & REFLECT

1. Immediately after Jesus' birth, we begin to see the enemy's plan at work. Who was partnering with the enemy to attempt to thwart the salvation plans of God the Father? (Of course, we know that no one can stop the plans of God.)

2. When the wise men reached Jesus, what was their immediate action?

3. Joseph moved his family several times during Jesus' early life. Why? In other words, how did this further God the Father's plan?

DECEMBER 17TH

Luke 2:1-7

http://bit.ly/ADOREadore

RESPOND & REFLECT

1. How do you think Mary and Joseph felt as they laid the baby Jesus, the Son of God, in a manger, a feeding trough?

2. What was God the Father's purpose in allowing His One and Only Son to be born in a stable and laid in a manger when He could've chosen any other place on earth for this baby King?

O COME
LET US
ADORE
HIM

DECEMBER 18TH

Luke 2:8-20

http://bit.ly/ADOREsilentnight

RESPOND & REFLECT

1. We have read enough accounts thus far to realize that everyone's reaction to the angel's messages has been fear. Why do you think that is?

2. According to the multitude of angels, what was Jesus' birth to bring to His people "on earth" (verse 14)?

3. As all these visitors kept coming and going, we don't have much recorded about Mary. What we do have says a lot about her. What does Luke tell us about her in verse 19? What significance does that bit of insight hold for us?

DECEMBER 19TH

Luke 2:21-24

http://bit.ly/ADOREachristmasalleluia

RESPOND & REFLECT

1. According to verse 21, when was the baby named?

2. Look up Leviticus 12:8. What can we infer about Mary and Joseph, knowing that they offered two turtledoves or young pigeons instead of a lamb?

3. Ironically, though Mary and Joseph may not have been able to afford a lamb for sacrifice, they were spiritually wealthy enough to be chosen to birth and raise THE Lamb - the Lamb of God. What character traits do we see in them that would have caused God the Father to choose them as Jesus' earthly parents?

DECEMBER 20TH

Luke 2:25-40

http://bit.ly/ADOREawayinamanger

RESPOND & REFLECT

1. What name of Jesus is highlighted in verse 26?

2. Simeon's words are important here. He prophesies about the purpose of this Baby. Look closely at verse 30. What is Jesus' purpose?

3. What is Anna's immediate reaction - two things actually - when she sees Jesus (verse 38)?

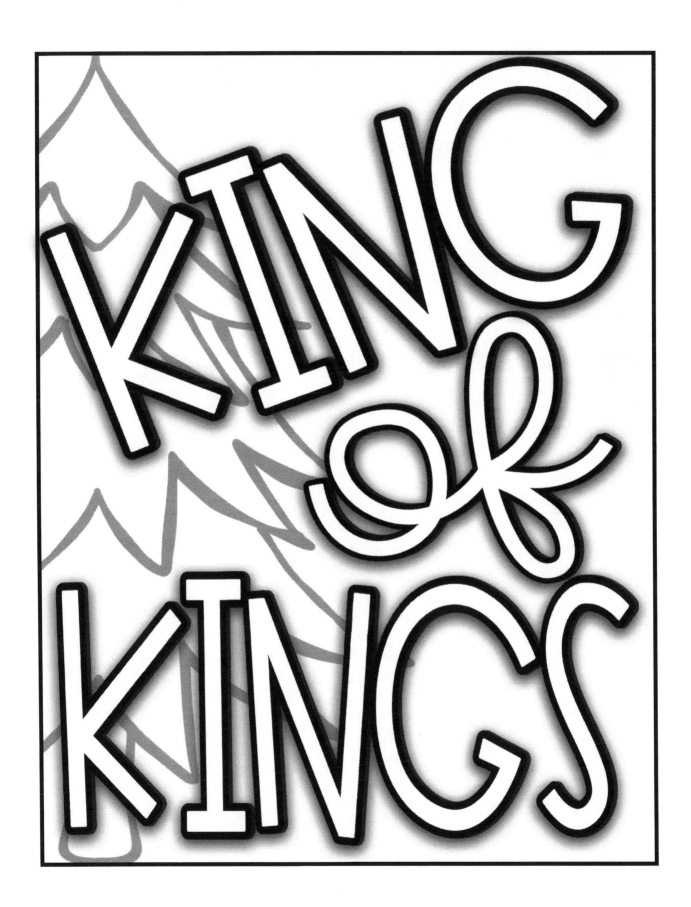

DECEMBER 21ST

Take time today for rest and reflection. If you need to catch up in the reading plan, today would be a good day for that. You can use the box below to jot down things that God has shown you in His word this week.

this week...

IN HIM
we have
REST

DECEMBER 22ND

- [ ] Psalm 86:15
- [ ] Ephesians 2:4-5
- [ ] 1 John 4:9-12

http://bit.ly/ADOREthegloryofchristmas

RESPOND & REFLECT

1. List 4 attributes of God that are found in Psalm 86:15.

2. The connection between God's mercy and His love keeps coming up in numerous passages. We see it again in Ephesians 2. How do you think His mercy and love connect?

3. According to 1 John, what should our response be to God's love?

Because of Jesus we have Love

DECEMBER 23RD

Mark 10:42-45

http://bit.ly/ADOREastrangewaytosavetheworld

RESPOND & REFLECT

1. Mark 10 jumps a bit further into Jesus' life. These 4 verses hold great truths from the mouth of our Savior. What does He tell James and John about those who want to be great (verses 43-44)?

2. The Son of Man spoken about in verse 45 is Jesus. According to Mark's record here, why did Jesus come?

3. Knowing this about our Savior should evoke what kind of response and/or application from us?

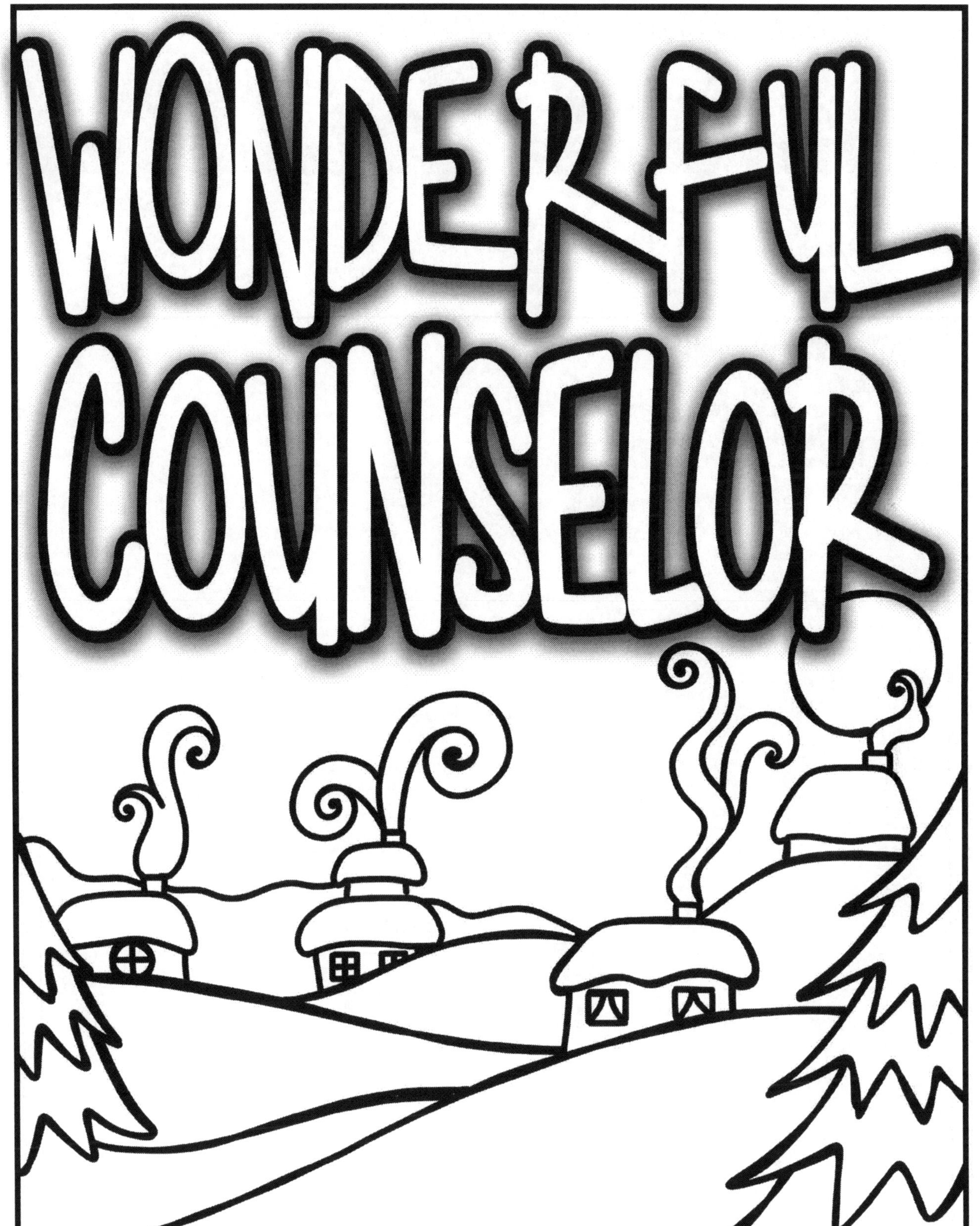
WONDERFUL
COUNSELOR

DECEMBER 24TH

John 14:26-28

http://bit.ly/ADOREhallelujahlighthascome

RESPOND & REFLECT

1. Jesus is speaking with His disciples in these verses. Who does He tell them will come when He goes away - back to Heaven?

2. What does Jesus tell them He is leaving with them (verse 27)? Why do you think this would have been a valuable reminder for them?

3. What hope does verse 27 offer to us?

SLEEP in heavenly PEACE

MERRY CHRISTMAS

☐ Galatians 4:4-7

☐ Philippians 2:1-11

RESPOND & REFLECT

1. Since Jesus was born *under* the law yet came to redeem those *under* the law, what does that tell us about His relation *to* the law?

2. What does Jesus offer us according to Galatians 4:5b?

3. Galatians 4:7 shouts some amazing news for us this Christmas Day...and every day! Read verse 7 as many times as you need and then explain what encouragement that verse holds for you personally today.

DECEMBER 26TH

☐ Luke 23

☐ Luke 24

http://bit.ly/ADOREjoytotheworld

RESPOND & REFLECT

1. Jesus' birth is not what brought salvation. It was His death and resurrection. Our sins needed payment, and His death was the payment for our sins: past, present, and future. Amazingly, and almost immediately following His death, a centurion realized what he had taken part in. What did the centurion confess in Luke 23:47?

2. Luke 24:6 holds words that separates Christianity from all other religions. What did the angels at the tomb say to those seeking Jesus (verse 6a)?

3. Jesus explains Himself to His disciples when He briefly returns to earth after His death and resurrection. What does He tell them in Luke 24:45-48?

DECEMBER 27TH

Matthew 28

http://bit.ly/ADOREgotellitonthemountain

RESPOND & REFLECT

1. The simile (comparison using like or as) used in verse 3 is one we heard in Isaiah 1:18. The Bible's words are 100% inspired - from the mouth of God. By using this comparison, what do you think Matthew is emphasizing about Jesus? In other words, Jesus came to do what for us?

2. Just like Anna in Luke 2 who saw Jesus and immediately ran to tell others about Him, Jesus has left us, His disciples, a similar command. According to verses 19-20, what is our job while we are here on earth?

3. What is one practical step can you take today to ensure that you are obeying Jesus' command?

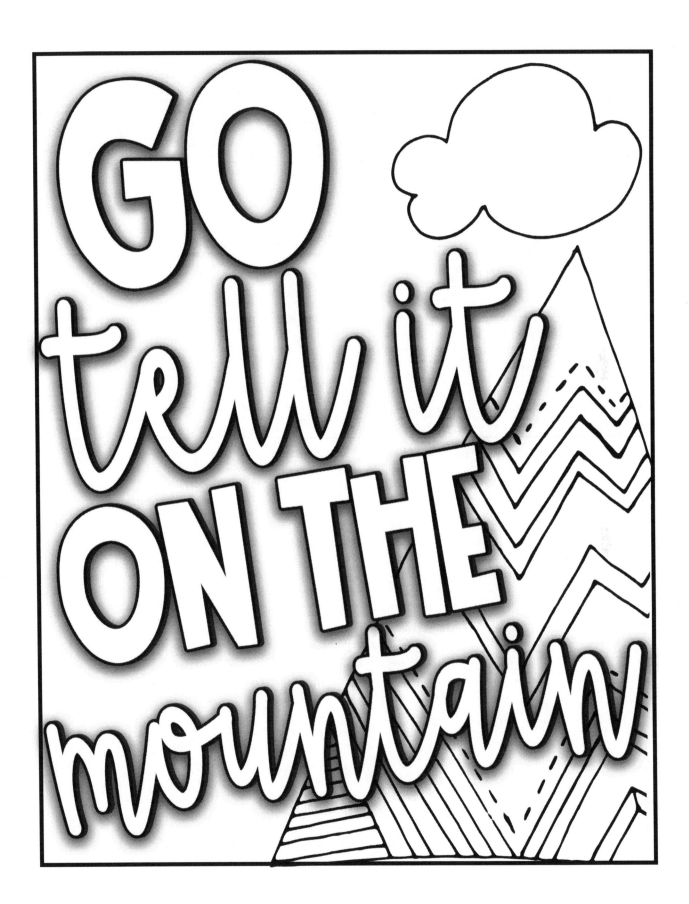

DECEMBER 28TH

Take time today for rest and reflection. If you need to catch up in the reading plan, today would be a good day for that. You can use the box below to jot down things that God has shown you in His word this week.

this week...

IN HIM we have REST

DECEMBER 29TH

☐ Mark 12:29-31   ☐ 1 Peter 4:8

☐ Romans 12:9-10   ☐ 1 John 3:16

☐ Ephesians 4:1-3

http://bit.ly/ADORErecklessloveofGod

RESPOND & REFLECT

1. All of these verses center around one theme, one command, that we have from Jesus as a result of what He did for us. According to Mark, what is the second greatest commandment?

2. How can you focus on Paul's command today to "outdo one another in showing honor"?

3. Jesus came to give us peace. Paul says in Ephesians that we should be *eager* to do what?

4. What is our ultimate display of love that mirrors our Savior's love for us according to 1 John?

DECEMBER 30TH

- [ ] Luke 6:38
- [ ] Galatians 6:2
- [ ] Philippians 2:3-4
- [ ] Hebrews 13:16

RESPOND & REFLECT

1. Not only are we to love one another, but we are also to serve one another. According to Luke, how are we to give?

2. How can you "look...to the interests of others" today as Paul encourages us to do in Philippians?

3. As we give and share and serve, what does God consider those (Hebrews 13:16)?

4. How is serving others a mirror of our Savior?

DECEMBER 31ST

- [ ] Matthew 5:44
- [ ] James 5:16
- [ ] Ephesians 6:18

RESPOND & REFLECT

1. Remember that Jesus' very birth brought nearly immediate pursuit and attempted persecution from one of His enemies, Herod. What is our response to be when others come against us and even persecute us? How is this mirroring Jesus?

2. James 5:16b has a powerful reminder about prayer for us. What is that reminder?

3. Who are we to pray for according to Paul in Ephesians?

CHRISTMAS PRAYERS

CHRISTMAS PRAYERS

CHRISTMAS PRAYERS

CHRISTMAS PRAYERS

CHRISTMAS PRAYERS

CHRISTMAS PRAYERS

CHRISTMAS PRAYERS

CHRISTMAS PRAYERS

CHRISTMAS PRAYERS

CHRISTMAS PRAYERS

OTHER RESOURCES BY TEACHERS IN THE Word

We, Bonnie and Bethany, both believe that interactive classrooms increase student engagement and learning. Come join our interactive classroom and explore a biblical world through QR Codes, coloring activities, and hands on activities in *Grace Changes Everything* and *Fruited.*

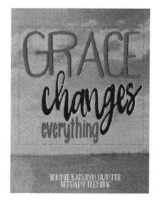

Come with us as we seek to dive deeper into God's Word and complete a 7-week study of the book of Ephesians. We believe that Grace Changes Everything. Grace changes marriages. Grace changes attitudes. Grace changes hearts and lives. Grace changes your classroom. Grace changes relationships. Join us as we study together and see how much grace can change you. We promise this Bible study is unlike any Bible study you have completed. This Bible study was specifically designed with the classroom teacher in mind. We are often asked how public school teachers can share Christ in their classrooms. While public school teachers may not be allowed to openly share Christ with their students, we believe that the love of Christ can be displayed through this word: Grace. You see, Paul was writing to the Ephesians who lived in a culture that was much like ours. The Ephesians had to be creative in order to spread Christ's love in an anti-Jesus culture. We will explore what grace looks like in our lives, homes, and classrooms. You will find practical application that you can take back to your classroom as you begin to live a grace filled life.

http://bit.ly/GRACECHANGESEVERYTHING

Come with us as we dive into God's Word and study the Fruit of the Spirit in Galatians 5. We will learn how to live a life that is rooted in Christ so that we can abound in fruit...it's #thefruitedlife, y'all! This study was written by teachers for teachers. Classroom stories and applications abound. This online 7-week study will be a great way to kick back, relax, and enjoy a glass of lemonade with teachers around the world as we laugh together, grow together, and learn together. You will find practical application that you can take back to your classroom as you begin to live the #fruitedlife.

http://bit.ly/FRUITED

FOLLOW US ON SOCIAL MEDIA

 @teachersintheword

 www.facebook.com/teachersintheword

 http://bit.ly/BonnieKathryn

 @bonniekathryn

 www.facebook.com/bonniekathrynclass

 Bonnie Kathryn Teaching

 @theenglishnerd

 The English Nerd

Terms of Use

Howard G. Hendricks, William D. Hendricks. *Living By the Book*. Chicago: Moody Publishers, 2007.

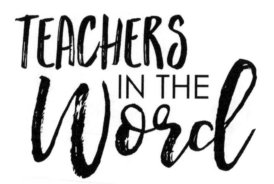

a ministry of

BONNIE KATHRYN
TEACHING

Author Credits:
Bethany Fleming
Bonnie Hunter

Made in the USA
Columbia, SC
22 November 2018